A WOMAN *of* GRACE

6 studies for individuals
or groups

Sandy Larsen

With Guidelines for Leaders
and Study Notes

 Women of Character Bible Studies

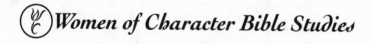

InterVarsity Press
Downers Grove, Illinois
Leicester, England

InterVarsity Press
P. O. Box 1400, Downers Grove, IL 60515, USA
38 De Montfort Street, Leicester LE1 7GP, England

InterVarsity Press® is the book-publishing division of InterVarsity Christian Fellowship®, a student movement active on campus at hundreds of universities, colleges and schools of nursing in the United States of America, and a member movement of the International Fellowship of Evangelical Students. For information about local and regional activities, write Public Relations Dept., InterVarsity Christian Fellowship, 6400 Schroeder Rd., P.O. Box 7895, Madison, WI 53707-7895.

Inter-Varsity Press, UK, is the book-publishing division of the Universities and Colleges Christian Fellowship (formerly the Inter-Varsity Fellowship), a student movement linking Christian Unions in universities and colleges throughout the United Kingdom and the Republic of Ireland, and a member movement of the International Fellowship of Evangelical Students. For information about local and national activities write to UCCF, 38 De Montfort Street, Leicester LE1 7GP.

USA ISBN 0-8308-2047-7

Cast of Characters

Setting the Stage

Each study's introduction takes the perspective of a different character in a continuing story to introduce the theme of each study. Below are the voices behind each introduction.

Katherine Fraley—mother of 3 teens, beginning a new job after not working outside the home for 15 years

Brad Fraley—Katherine's husband, unemployed for the last 10 months

Ms. Clyde—Katherine's supervisor at work

Shannon—Katherine's coworker

Phil—Katherine's coworker

Sarah—Katherine & Brad's daughter, 13

Theresa—Katherine & Brad's daughter, 15

Joel—Katherine & Brad's son, 12

Gillian—Shannon's daughter, 13

Introducing *A Woman of Grace*

She had tremendous stress. She experienced the pressure of making decisions and the equal pressure of having all decisions taken out of her hands. She was forced into unwanted roles. Yet stress did not overwhelm her. Through it all, her life showed inner serenity and grace.

As we dig into her story, we find the biblical character Esther a surprisingly contemporary woman. She faced many of the same obstacles and problems we face as Christian women living in a secular society.

She was a captive in a strange country where the king ruled absolutely. He could dismiss his queen with a word; he could order the nation's most beautiful women to be rounded up and forced to audition for his harem, to be summoned at his impulse. But Esther refused to play the role of helpless victim, though she had plenty of reasons to do so.

Life was stacked against Esther from the start. She was orphaned in a land of exile. Even after she was drafted into the role of queen, she held a glamorous yet powerless position under the king's domination. Yet Esther carried herself with such dignity, faith and confidence that she won over those around her.

She had the wisdom to know when to lay her life on the line for the people of God and when to hold back her words and actions. She carefully chose her risks. Esther's life is a balance of boldness and restraint.

She affected history by her faithfulness and obedience. Through her intervention, disaster for the people of God was turned into a victory celebration; loss was transformed into salvation.

If Esther sounds like superwoman, there is good reason for it. In her life there was more going on than the triumph of the human spirit. Throughout Esther's remarkable story, God is always at work behind the scenes: opening opportunities, arranging coincidences, protecting key players, revealing the right thing at the right time.

So we are more like Esther than we know. Like her, we were born into a culture not our own. That is true even if we still live in the town where we grew up. As Christians we live in this world, but we are loyal to another Lord beyond it. Our question is the same one that faced Esther: How should we live in this land of exile away from our true home?

We see wrongs being done. Are we willing to build credibility before we confront the people in power?

We see sin going on. Have we bothered to understand the sinners so in time of crisis we know how to approach them?

We see action that needs to be taken. Can we restrain ourselves at certain times so we can move boldly at the right times?

As we study the book of Esther, we will follow the story of a fictional woman, Kathleen, and her very contemporary struggles as a mom returning to the workplace. Yet Kathleen also faces many of the same ethical questions that Esther confronted. Kathleen's story will introduce each study and get you thinking about the topic at hand.

Esther, our surprising contemporary, is also our example: a woman of grace who knew who she was and what she could do in God's strength. And like Esther, we have the assurance that behind the scenes God is always working to accomplish his will.

Suggestions for Individual Study

1. As you begin each study pray that God will speak to you through his Word.

2. Read the introduction to the study, "Setting the Stage," and respond to the questions that follow it. The story is designed to draw you into the topic at hand and help you begin to see how the Scripture relates to daily life. If there will be a week or more between your studies, then you may want to read all of the introductions in one sitting to get the flow of the ongoing story. This will help if you find that you are having trouble keeping track of all the characters.

3. This is an inductive Bible study, designed to help you discover for yourself what Scripture is saying. Each study deals with a particular passage — so that you can really delve into the author's meaning in that context. Read and reread the passage to be studied. The questions are written using the language of the New International Version, so you may wish to use that version of the Bible. The New Revised Standard Version is also recommended.

4. "God's Word for Us" includes three types of questions. *Observation* questions ask about the basic facts: who, what, when, where and how. *Interpretation* questions delve into the meaning of the passage. *Application* questions (also found in the "Now or Later" section) help you discover the implications of the text for growing in Christ.

These three keys unlock the treasures of Scripture.

Write your answers to the study questions in the spaces provided or in a personal journal. Writing can bring clarity and deeper understanding of yourself and of God's Word.

5. Use the study notes at the back of the guide to gain additional insight and information after you have worked through the questions for yourself.

6. Move to the "Now or Later" section. These are ideas for you to freely use in closing your study and responding to God. You may want to choose one of these to do right away and continue working through the other ideas on subsequent days to reinforce what you are learning.

Suggestions for Members of a Group Study

1. Come to the study prepared. Follow the suggestions for individual study mentioned above. You will find that careful preparation will greatly enrich your time spent in group discussion.

2. Be willing to participate in the discussion. The leader of your group will not be lecturing. Instead, she will be encouraging the members of the group to discuss what they have learned. The leader will be asking the questions that are found in this guide.

3. Stick to the topic being discussed. Your answers should be based on the verses which are the focus of the discussion and not on outside authorities such as commentaries or speakers. These studies focus on a particular passage of Scripture. Only rarely should you refer to other portions of the Bible. This allows for everyone to participate on equal ground and for in-depth study.

4. Be sensitive to the other members of the group. Listen attentively when they describe what they have learned. You may be surprised by their insights! Each question assumes a variety of answers. Many questions do not have "right" answers, particularly questions that aim at meaning or application. Instead the questions push us to explore the passage more thoroughly.

When possible, link what you say to the comments of others. Also, be affirming whenever you can. This will encourage some of the more hesitant members of the group to participate.

5. Be careful not to dominate the discussion. We are sometimes so eager to express our thoughts that we leave too little opportunity for others to respond. By all means participate! But allow others to also.

6. Expect God to teach you through the passage being discussed and through the other members of the group. Pray that you will have an enjoyable and profitable time together, but also that as a result of the study, you will find ways that you can take action individually and/or as a group.

7. It will be helpful for groups to follow a few basic guidelines. These guidelines, which you may wish to adapt to your situation, should be read at the beginning of the first session.

☐ Anything said in the group is considered confidential and will not be discussed outside the group unless specific permission is given to do so.

☐ We will provide time for each person present to talk if he or she feels comfortable doing so.

☐ We will talk about ourselves and our own situations, avoiding conversation about other people.

☐ We will listen attentively to each other.

☐ We will be very cautious about giving advice.

☐ We will pray for each other.

8. If you are the group leader, you will find additional suggestions at the back of the guide.

1

..

The Grace of Inner Beauty

Esther 2:1-14

 SETTING THE STAGE

Katherine Fraley stood facing the battered metal door, weighing her options and shuffling her feet. On the other side of that door she would apply for a new job. After fifteen years of being a full-time mom, applying for any job was scary enough. What made it even harder was that this job — stuffing ad inserts in the local shopper — was far below her abilities and education.

The door popped open and a young woman, maybe fifteen years younger than Katherine, slouched out chomping a big red wad of gum. The girl collided with Katherine and moved down the hall without even saying "Excuse me."

Another happy employee, Katherine thought. *If that's the kind of people who work here ... What if that's the boss!*

I can't allow myself to think like this. I should thank the Lord there's even the possibility of work.

Katherine remembered the look on Brad's face as she left the house that morning. In one way he was getting harder to read, less accessible. In another way she could read him better all the time. Unemployment was wearing on him more every day. The layoff was ten months ago. He didn't object to her working, but it hurt his pride to think his wife might become the sole support of the family.

Standing straighter and taking a deep breath, Katherine opened the door and walked into the office. She told the bored-looking receptionist, "I'd like to apply for the job that was in the paper."

"Yeah. Sure. Fill this out."

Katherine took the application, sat down and tried to compress who she was into those cramped spaces on the form. A skeleton of data: name, address, social security number. Previous work experience. Hmm. Chef, chauffeur, repair person, nurse, home decorator, neighborhood counselor, referee . . . She handed back the paper, knowing it was a pathetic caricature of her true self. She was surprised when the receptionist said, "Ms. Clyde can talk to you now." An interview already?

Ms. Clyde motioned Katherine to sit down as she scanned the application. Katherine watched the eyes, watched the hard face, wanted to interrupt, "What I've written there is not the real me! The real me is going to be an English teacher!" The face of Ms. Clyde dissolved into the face of Katherine's college roommate. It was the end of their junior year, and they were talking late into the night.

"Sure, I understand why you're marrying Brad now," her roommate said. "But why can't he hang around here for a year while you finish college?"

Katherine explained for the twentieth time, "He's graduating and has this job offer in another town, and we want a family right away. There's a small college near there. When the kids are older, I can go back and finish my degree and get my teaching certificate."

Her friend looked skeptical. "Listen, Katherine, if you don't finish your degree now, I'll guarantee you'll never get around to it."

Katherine proceeded according to plan, marrying Brad the week after he graduated. She did office work that first year before Theresa was born. Sarah and Joel soon followed. Katherine was always busy, and Brad's career looked secure. As the degree seemed less and less important, she somehow never got around to going back to college. Finally when the kids were fifteen, thirteen and twelve, no longer rushing home after school expecting Mom to be there, the time seemed right.

Then disaster hit. Brad's company went through a big merger and layoff. After his first flurry of job-hunting, they both realized their small college town didn't have enough jobs to absorb all the newly unemployed.

Katherine was pulled back to reality as Ms. Clyde announced, "You're overqualified." Katherine wanted to shout, "You bet I am!" She also wanted to break into tears and plead, "But I've got to have a job of some kind!" Instead of doing either, she silently prayed and then answered, "I know I can do this job well for you."

The other woman's face thawed out slightly. She asked Katherine a few more questions, gave her a couple of brief tests and said, "All right. Come back Monday and we'll start training you."

Katherine stumbled out. *I'm hired!* She looked back at the grungy door. *Here?* How would she explain this to people? Yes, this job was an answer to prayer. Through this work the Lord would provide for the Fraley family till Brad found something and life got back to normal. Katherine knew she should be ecstatic, but she wished the Lord had answered some other way.

---

1. When have you been forced into circumstances you didn't want?

---

2. What factors make Katherine's situation particularly difficult?

 GOD'S WORD FOR US
Read Esther 2:1-14.
Background: The first chapter of the book of Esther relates how King Ahasuerus (Xerxes) of Persia grew disenchanted with his queen Vashti. She refused to be paraded before drunken nobility as part of Xerxes' display of wealth. Following the suggestion of his advisors, the king deposed Vashti. When he calmed down, he apparently realized he needed someone to take her place.

---

3. Summarize the king's plan for acquiring a new queen (vv. 1-4).

4. What can you find out about the young Jewish girl Esther from verses 5-7?

5. How had God blessed Esther and taken care of her up until the time she was selected for the king's harem?

6. Even before she was forcibly taken to the king's palace, Esther had many reasons to feel that her life had been difficult and unfair. Are there any ways in which you share her feelings? Consider the following factors.

Orphaned

Raised by an older cousin

Exiled in a foreign culture with radically different morals

7. When Xerxes' order went out, Esther attracted attention and was taken in as part of the royal collection of potential queens. How did God continue to take care of her in the king's harem, where she appeared to be only a glamorous slave (vv. 8-11)?

8. Each young woman in Xerxes' harem received a year of beauty treatments before being sent to the king (v. 12). During that year, why would it have been difficult for a godly woman to focus on inner beauty and character?

9. How might Esther have kept and even developed her inner beauty while everything around her was focused on the external?

10. When do you find it most difficult to conduct yourself with dignity and grace, even when you need both to get you through a tough situation?

NOW OR LATER

Ideas to close your group meeting or personal study or for continued daily reflection.

☐ Take time to think and write about your memories of undergoing stress. What qualities of your inner life (good or bad) have been revealed at those times? If you recall qualities you aren't proud of, how would the grace of inner beauty have helped you to respond differently?

☐ God is not named in the book of Esther. Yet on every page he is there, just as he is our unseen helper in our most helpless moments. When Esther was under tremendous pressure, God brought the right people into her life. Identify times when God put the right people in the right places to help you. Name each person and explain how that person's help was just what you needed at that time.

☐ For further study read John 14. Note how on his last night with his disciples before he died, Jesus promised: "The world will not see me anymore, but you will see me. Because I live, you also will live" (John 14:19). Bring your most overwhelming situation to Christ and let him be your unseen Helper. Resolve to live tomorrow and each succeeding day depending on his grace.

2

···

The Grace of Consistency

Esther 2:15-23

 SETTING THE STAGE

Layers of newspaper ink—years' worth—were ground into the cement floor and walls of the room where Katherine worked. The lighting was utilitarian and harsh. But when she stewed inwardly about the atmosphere of the place, it was the human element that bothered her more than the bleak physical surroundings.

The atmosphere here is terrible, she thought. *No, terrible is too strong a word. The atmosphere is . . . non-uplifting. It's not very positive. It's rather cynical. Well, yes, it's terrible.*

Nobody could accuse Katherine's coworkers of lacking team spirit. They spoke with one voice about several matters: life was rotten, their spouses or partners were impossible to live with, this stuffing room was the world's worst place to work.

Most of all they were united in their opinion of their supervisor, Ms. Clyde. To her face they were politely neutral. Behind her back they called her all kinds of things Katherine didn't want to repeat. Leading the anti-

Clyde forces were Shannon and Phil, who had work stations on either side of Katherine. They enjoyed depicting Ms. Clyde as the workplace witch.

At home Katherine let off steam by exploding to Brad. "I hate that place! All everybody does there all day is gripe and complain. They're the crabbiest people I've ever had to be around!"

Brad looked pained. "Hey, things are rough enough. Do me a favor, will you, and don't become a griper!"

While Katherine silently fumed, thinking, *It's bad enough I have to work there, now I have to put on a smiley face and not talk about it,* Brad seemed to read her thoughts. "What I mean is, it's helped me a lot that you've stayed upbeat. I hate to see you lose that."

The next day at work Katherine told a couple of stories about amusing things that had happened in her family. She talked about her church. She suggested that Ms. Clyde had a lot of pressures on her. In response, her fellow workers treated Katherine like a visitor from another planet—someone who was out of touch with the real world.

One day Katherine came in to find the place in an unusually elated mood. Shannon and Phil, surrounded by some of their cohorts, were actually laughing. They shut down as soon as they noticed Katherine. "Don't tell her," someone hissed. But later that day Shannon couldn't resist bragging how they finally had the goods on their supervisor. They planned to go to the higher-ups and lodge certain complaints about Ms. Clyde which had no basis in reality.

Katherine tried to ignore it. She told herself it was none of her business and it would only complicate things if she got involved. She reminded herself that she wasn't so fond of Ms. Clyde either. But the unfairness of it nagged at her. No one else was going to stick up for the supervisor.

One day during their brief lunch break, Katherine drew Shannon aside. "This plan you and Phil have been talking about," she began, "lodging those complaints — are you really sure it's the best thing to do?"

"What's it to you?" Shannon demanded.

"Well — nothing," Katherine said. "Except that . . ."

"You're going to be the goody-goody around here, is that it?"

"No, but — it just bothers me to see something done that isn't based on facts. That's all. It would be one thing if there were valid complaints about her work or her honesty, but when it's just — well — a personality clash. . . ."

Shannon was looking closely at Katherine. This time her look said more than "What planet are you from?" It said "You're dangerous." Katherine wondered if she should have said so much, but what's done was done, and she would deal with the conequences.

---

1. What does Katherine risk by acting in a way that is consistent with her Christian faith?

---

2. What does she risk by not acting in a way that is consistent with her Christian faith?

GOD'S WORD FOR US
Read Esther 2:15-23.

3. What were the steps of Esther's elevation to the position of Vashti's replacement as Xerxes' queen (vv. 15-18)?

4. In the headiness of her new and glamorous position, Esther could have been swept into naively accepting whatever came her way. Throughout this passage, what evidence do you find of Esther's discernment about whose advice to take?

Person She Trusted   **Evidence**

5. Mordecai learned some volatile information (vv. 21-22). What was it, and what did he choose to do with it?

6. What did the king find out about Esther's character through her actions (v. 22)?

7. Esther and Mordecai had the despotic king's life in their hands. They could have thought of several reasons to stand by and let the plot be carried out. How was their intervention both compassionate and wise?

---

8. When have you had the opportunity to act in a consistent Christian way toward someone you had reason to resent? What happened?

---

9. How is consistency a reflection of God's character?

---

10. How would you grade your own trustworthiness?

---

11. In what areas of your life would you like to be more consistent and trustworthy?

Now or Later

☐ When Esther reported the assassination plot to the king, she proved that both she and Mordecai could be trusted. When she made her report, it was more than a PR move. She was not simply enhancing her image of trustworthiness; she was being trustworthy. Consistency earns us the reputation of credibility. How much credibility do you think you have with your community?

with family members?

at work?

in volunteer organizations, including the church?

Examine your conscience and ask the Lord to identify any ways in which you are not trustworthy, such as: betraying confidences

not following through on things you promised to do

dishonesty, or evading the truth

☐ Besides being trustworthy herself, Esther was wise about who else was trustworthy. Are you struggling to know who can be trusted? Maybe you've trusted people in the past and were disappointed when they proved untrustworthy. "If any of you lacks wisdom, he should ask God, who gives generously to all without finding fault, and it will be given to him" (James 1:5). Pray for wisdom to know whom to trust with sensitive information or delicate situations.

Thank the Lord for people you can trust. Recall times you confided in them or took their advice with good results. Praise God for their Christlikeness and take them for your example.

□ For further study read Psalm 27. Note each of David's expressions of confidence in the Lord. Remember that the Lord is absolutely trustworthy. He can be told anything in strictest confidence—he is unshockable—and, best of all, he has all wisdom and can counsel you about what to do next.

3

....

The Grace to Stand for God

Esther 3:1-11

 SETTING THE STAGE

Monday morning again. It was hard enough for Katherine to face going to work without what hit her when she walked in. Shannon announced loudly, "Here comes Ms. Holiness!"

Katherine tried to make light of it. She looked behind her, searching in vain for Ms. Holiness. "Are you talking about me?"

"Well, nobody else around here qualifies, do they?"

Once they were at their work stations, Katherine got busy stuffing papers and Shannon got down to the point. She leaned toward Katherine and said quietly but intensely, "You ratted on us! You did it because of your religion, right?"

It didn't matter that Katherine was too startled to answer, because Shannon was still talking. "You went to Clyde and blabbed everything. Phil says she knows all about what we were going to do."

"Of course I didn't go to her!" Katherine shot back.

But Shannon wasn't finished. "Now you've got Phil and me and some other people in hot water. She thinks we were trying to get her fired."

Lord, how should I defend myself? "Shannon, I didn't say anything to her. I only talked to you because I thought I should say something."

That was the hook Shannon was waiting for. Her voice escalated. "You church people are always poking your nose into other people's business! Why can't you keep your religion to yourself?"

Good question! Katherine wondered the same thing. *If only I'd stayed in my comfortable circle of church and family and neighborhood. If only I hadn't gotten into this crazy place among these strange people. Never mind that Brad is out of work, it would have been better to —*

Shannon interrupted Katherine's thoughts with a warning. Her voice was full of exaggerated concern. "I'd watch out for Phil if I were you. He doesn't care who he shoots down. What he can do to one person he can do to another. You may be next."

So blame it all on Phil, is that it? Make him the ringleader? So what can he do to me? Get me fired? I'd love it! No, maybe I wouldn't, because we still need this job.

If there was any doubt that Katherine was in the doghouse with Phil, he erased it later that day when he called out to her, "So did you help old Clyde get religion? When are you two leaving for your world cruise together? I hear you're on buddy-buddy terms." That was one of the nicer things he said to her all afternoon. Other people at work were even colder to her than usual. The word was out: Katherine was the new office scapegoat. It was all because of something she didn't do, and it was mixed up with her being a Christian.

Katherine thought, *Well, I sure can't write any books on how to win friends and influence people. I tried to do the right thing and I made enemies. Lord, you'll have to be my defender. I'll stick it out. I don't want to become like these people. But I won't quit this place until you tell me to.*

---

1. How have Katherine's motives been confused and misrepresented?

---

2. As Katherine tries to maintain her Christian witness in this hostile atmosphere, what do you think is most important for her to remember about the Lord?

about herself?

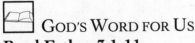 GOD'S WORD FOR US
Read Esther 3:1-11.

---

3. How was Mordecai different from the other palace officials (vv. 2-4)?

4. The other officials, trying to protect Mordecai or trying to avoid trouble, begged Mordecai to comply with the king's command. What explanation had Mordecai given them for refusing to bow to Haman (v. 4)?

_____

5. How did Haman inflate his hatred of Mordecai (vv. 5-7)?

_____

6. How did Haman enlist the king's endorsement of his plan (vv. 8-9)?

_____

7. Because Haman hated Mordecai, he went after all the Jews in Xerxes' kingdom. When have you been the object of someone's wrath simply through "guilt by association"?

_____

8. What are some ways that Christians today are targeted for criticism?

9. When we hear Christian faith attacked, most of us get defensive. Perhaps we leap to our own defense even more than to the defense of Christ. How do you typically respond to unreasonable opposition to your faith?

10. If you came to faith in Christ in your teens or adulthood, recall any negative feelings you had about Christians before then. How do your memories help you understand people today who find fault with Christians?

11. How would you like to change the ways you respond to unreasonable opposition?

 NOW OR LATER

☐ Write about your experiences with people who have gone above and beyond the call of duty in opposing your faith in Christ. Detail how you felt about those people and anything that helped you have a more Christlike attitude toward them, such as coming to understand their background, listening to their hurts, forgiving them, or feeling new compassion for them.

☐ Pray specifically by name for the people who are giving you the most opposition because of your faith.

☐ Confess to the Lord any ways that you may deserve the opposition (by unChristlike attitudes and actions, for example). Talk to another person about this if it's appropriate.

☐ For further study read 1 Peter 3:8-17. Decide now how you will react the next time you come under attack for your faith. (Keeping silent and doing nothing can be a legitimate reaction.)

Pray that you'll have a Christlike attitude toward those who oppose you, showing compassion without compromising your beliefs.

4

The Grace to Take Risks

Esther 4:1-14

 SETTING THE STAGE

It was Saturday morning, and the sun's warmth was soaking the air and the earth. A great day to be outdoors, especially after spending all week in an ink-saturated stuffing room. Katherine was on her knees in the yard, digging in the warm dirt, pulling weeds. Even while she worked, the faces of the people at the shopper moved through her mind. Many of them had turned against her, but she found herself wondering what was going on inside them.

On the front lawn Brad played catch with Joel. The layoff had certainly given him more time to spend with the kids. Theresa, their fifteen-year-old, came out of the house with two of her church friends. They were all munching fresh-baked cookies. Since Katherine started working, Theresa had taken over some kitchen duties and no longer expected Mom to do it all. It was good preparation for when Katherine went back to school—which she still believed was in her future, though not as soon as she'd hoped.

Katherine got to her feet and asked, "Where's Sarah?" Their thirteen-year-old had talked about going shopping with some other girls. Katherine and Brad were concerned that lately Sarah had been gravitating toward the wrong friends.

Brad fired the ball to Joel, who caught it handily and then dropped a bombshell. "Her friend Gillian called and they went to Gillian's house to watch movies. I heard them talking." He obviously envied the coup his big sister had pulled off.

If Sarah had a friend named Gillian, this was the first Katherine had heard of it. *Sarah is off at some stranger's house, and we didn't even notice when she left! How could this happen? It's the job. It's not being there when the kids come home from school. It's . . . Calm down.*

An hour or so later Sarah tooled up on her bike, well-prepared for the fallout. Her face and demeanor were carefully nonchalant and her guard was up as she sat in the kitchen peeling an orange.

"I told Theresa where I was going," she claimed. Theresa denied it, but maybe she hadn't heard her little sister. Joel piped up that Sarah and Gillian planned to watch about fifty movies. He started naming their titles. Brad told him to go outside, then explained, "Sarah, those movies aren't ones we want you watching. You know that."

"Gillian's mother lets her watch those movies all the time."

Katherine asked, "Was Gillian's mother there?"

"Yeah. She was sleeping."

"How about her dad?" Brad asked. "Was he there?"

"Yeah," Sarah answered, "only he's not really her dad. He's moving out soon. Look, you always tell me to be friendly to kids who don't go to church. I'm not supposed to only have Christian friends. Right?"

Determined to stick to the point, Katherine responded, "But your dad and I want to know where you are and who you're with. We don't know these people yet."

Sarah looked very surprised. "Sure you do, Mom. Gillian's mother works at the same place you do. Her name's Shannon."

That night when they were alone, Brad told Katherine, "You're the one to talk to Shannon about this. You know her and I don't."

"But what do I tell her? She already thinks I'm a prude and a goody-goody. Now do I tell her we don't want her daughter to be friends with our daughter?"

"Well . . . do we want Sarah to be friends with this Gillian?"

"I don't know. I know I don't want the two of them watching movies unsupervised. Or even supervised by Shannon."

"Maybe this is your chance to really explain our values," Brad suggested. "I know, I know, that's easy for me to say. You're the one who has to walk in there and face her. But maybe this is why the Lord has you working right next to this Shannon."

---

1. What are some pros and cons of Katherine talking to Shannon about the movies and the girls' friendship?

2. When have you felt you were "the one" to take on a particularly difficult assignment?

 GOD'S WORD FOR US

Read Esther 4:1-14.

Background: The king agreed to Haman's scheme against the Jews, not knowing that it would put Queen Esther's life in danger. Xerxes issued the terrible order of genocide throughout Persia. All the Jews would be annihilated on a particular day (see 3:12-15).

3. How did Mordecai and the other Jews react to news of the king's order (vv. 1-3)?

4. Esther was mystified and upset by Mordecai's strange behavior. What do you think about what she did first (v. 4)?

5. When Mordecai refused Esther's offer of clean clothes, she pursued an answer about his actions (vv. 5-8). How

did Mordecai urge Esther to get involved in the Jews'
dilemma?

6. Why did Esther hesitate to comply with Mordecai's
urging (vv. 9-11)?

7. How did Mordecai make his case that Esther had to
get involved (vv. 12-14)?

8. How do you react when someone tells you that you
ought to do something (especially that you're *the* person
to do something)?

___ I feel it's a message from God, and I try to obey.

___ I feel inadequate to do what I'm being asked to do.

___ I don't mind, because I need a push to do the right thing.

___ I give in easily, usually out of guilt.

___ I resent the other person trying to control my life.

___ I believe God chooses specific people for specific jobs;
I just don't always know if I'm really the one.

___ Another reason:

9. Where are you in conflict about whether (or how much) to get involved with something that could be highly inconvenient for you?

---

10. God put Esther in a particular situation in order to carry out his purposes there through her. How has God used you in the place where you live, work or go to school? Think of things that have happened because you were in a particular place at a particular time.

 NOW OR LATER

☐ Like Esther, we are where we are not by accident but by design. For each of us, "such a time as this" is right now. But where we are—position, role, sphere of influence—is different for each person. Reflect on possible reasons why God has put you where you are.

Place:

Time of life:

Family status:

Responsibilities:

Abilities:

Important relationships:

Praise God for his purposes in your life. Acknowledge his plans for you and renew your commitment to following him.

☐ If you are not sure—or have no idea—why you are where you are, put the details of your life before God. Ask him for enlightenment about your mission. God's answer will probably not come in a flash but in a gradual unfolding of events.

☐ For further study read Genesis 50:15-21, concentrating on verse 20. Joseph's brothers begged him to forgive them for selling him into slavery in Egypt. Joseph had the longer view and saw God working out his purposes even in his brothers' cruelty and rejection.

5

The Grace to Have Courage

Esther 4:15 — 5:8

 SETTING THE STAGE

The Ms. Clyde Caper and Phil's Revenge had diminished in Katherine's mind by the time she went to work on Monday. She was thinking only of what she would say to Shannon, who had taken on a new identity as Gillian's mother.

Shannon's attitude toward Katherine was sullen but no different from last week. Apparently she didn't keep track of Gillian's friends.

All morning Katherine wondered how to approach her coworker. She rehearsed her reasons for not wanting Sarah to watch those movies and why she preferred that the girls come to Sarah's house. But how would Shannon respond? Finally toward noon she swallowed her fear and said, "Shannon, could I talk to you about something?"

"Not about your religion," Shannon snapped.

The comment, like the slamming of a door, said volumes that Katherine hadn't heard before. With a quick prayer for wisdom, Katherine shifted her approach. "What are you doing after work?" she asked. "How about going for coffee or a sandwich or something? My family can take care of themselves for one evening!"

Katherine refrained from laughing at the expression on Shannon's face. *My face must have looked like that when Sarah told me you're Gillian's mother,* she thought.

After work Katherine dashed in the door. "Pray for me, will you?" she asked Brad. "I'm just going to change clothes and go meet Shannon."

"Okay. Pray for me," Brad replied. "I got a call from Sims Company. Remember I applied there and hadn't heard anything? Well, there's an opening now. I'm interviewing on Thursday!"

Katherine nearly danced out the door. For a moment her fear of Shannon was forgotten.

Over soup and a sandwich, Katherine launched her appeal. "Did you know that your daughter and my daughter are friends? My daughter is Sarah. She was over at your house Saturday."

"Oh, yeah, Gillie said she had somebody over. I was asleep. You know I work another job weekend nights."

"You do? I didn't know that."

"Yeah. I'd like to quit it, but I can't since her dad's one of those deadbeats who doesn't pay me what he's supposed to."

Katherine took a spoonful of soup and then a bite of sandwich to give herself time to think. She had never considered that Shannon's life might be tough. No wonder she constantly complained—she had real hurts. Was it time yet to bring up the subject of movies? No, not yet.

"How long has it been since you were divorced?" she asked.

"Huh? Oh, we're not divorced. We were never married. I wanted to get married but he didn't. It's a long story."

Yes, a very long story. Too long for this conversation. "Shannon, Brad and I really want to know the families of our kids' friends. Why don't you and Gillie come over some time? The adults can visit, and the girls can—watch movies. We've got some really good movies that . . ." Katherine was stumbling. It was okay. She'd explain more about their values when Shannon was in their home.

Shannon looked at Katherine a moment as if trying to figure her out. Then she shrugged. "Sure. I never go anywhere—just work all the time." Her eyes narrowed. "Old Clyde won't be there, will she?"

---

1. What do you think of the wisdom of Katherine's approach to Shannon?

---

2. What strategies has God led you to use to approach people in touchy situations?

 GOD'S WORD FOR US
Read Esther 4:15—5:8.

---

3. How did Esther plan to prepare herself for the challenge of going in to see the king unannounced (4:15-16)?

4. What does the fact that she enlisted help from others tell you about Esther?

_____

5. How would you paraphrase Esther's statement "And if I perish, I perish" (4:16)?

_____

6. Does Esther's statement strike you as faith or fatalism? Why?

_____

7. Compare Esther's response to crisis with your own response:

__ Like Esther, I hesitate to do anything until I have other people's prayer support.
__ I don't take action until I have clear guidance from God.
__ I act impulsively, sometimes forgetting to pray first.
__ I often hang back in fear; I wish I had more faith.
__ I avoid dealing with crises; I just hope they'll go away.
__ Other:

_____

8. What was the outcome of Esther's unannounced appearance before the king (5:1-3)?

9. When the king offered to grant Esther any request she made, we would expect her to immediately beg him to cancel his order against the Jews. Instead, she invited him to two banquets. What reasons might she have had for putting the king off (5:4, 8)?

_____

10. In her approach to the king, Esther displayed a balance of caution and courage. What unfortunate results can come from caution without courage?

courage without caution?

_____

11. When the Lord calls you to a special task, are you more prone to react with courage (minus caution) or caution (minus courage)?

_____

12. For what situation right now do you need the right mixture of courage and caution?

NOW OR LATER

☐ In some area of your life the Lord is calling you to obey him in faith. Obedience may not mean risking your physical life as Esther did, but it is bound to cost you something in time, convenience, status, finances and/or energy.

Identify the challenge which God is placing before you. Spell out the risks, just as Esther did to Mordecai. Naming your fears can take some of the dread out of them.

If you don't think you are ready yet to meet the challenge, honestly lay your attitude before the Lord. Consider the strategy and approach you would use if you were ready. Tell God you are willing to have your mind and heart changed. Thank him for his mercy and patience.

If you feel ready and willing to meet the challenge, tell the Lord so and ask for his grace to carry out what you need to do. Enlist the prayer support of others in your group, or make plans to enlist others' prayer support.

Write out and prayerfully consider the first step toward meeting this challenge.

Make a list of possible results.

Plan for a possible next step, depending on which of those results happens.

☐ For further study read 2 Timothy 1:3-12. Paul apparently sensed that his young protégé Timothy was struggling with fear. His words to Timothy can be God's words to us now and in any frightening situation.

6

The Grace to See God's Faithfulness

Esther 7:1 — 8:2

 SETTING THE STAGE

Two weeks later Katherine arrived at work in the best mood ever. She said hello to Shannon, who even smiled at her a little. She said hello to Phil, who grumbled something back. It didn't matter now. Katherine's remaining days here were few, and she was ecstatic. *College, here I come.*

The first chance she got, Katherine talked to her supervisor. "Ms. Clyde, I'm giving my notice. My husband has a new job. We won't be moving, because it's right here in town. We're really happy about it. It's —"

"Okay," the supervisor said abruptly. Just what Katherine expected from her. Well, it didn't matter. Only two more weeks and . . . what was that? "Excuse me, Ms. Clyde?"

"I said I'll miss you around here. You're a good worker."

"Oh — well — thank you. I have to say it's been . . . interesting to work here."

"You sure you can't stay on at least part-time? We could work something out."

Stay on at this place? Are you kidding?

Ms. Clyde continued, "Maybe three days a week or something like that. We're flexible around here. You know, I think you bring a little life to this place."

Life? Katherine mentally stepped outside herself and saw the stick-in-the-mud who never laughed at the jokes. Did she really bring something fresh and wholesome into this atmosphere?

"Something on the bright side, I mean," Ms. Clyde went on. "Working at this place can be a drag, you know that?"

"Uh . . . yes, I suppose it could be, if you let it."

"You're different from the others. You're not a griper. Think about it and we'll talk about it later, all right?" She looked directly at Katherine, and a protective veil seemed to have fallen away from her eyes. "I'd appreciate it."

"Thank you, Ms. Clyde. I can think about it, I guess," Katherine said. She stumbled out, much as she'd stumbled out the day she applied for work here. *I'm not a griper? Lord, what if I had been? What if I'd been like all the others?*

Maybe God had send her here precisely for these people right now. Certainly for Shannon and Gillian. Maybe for Ms. Clyde. Maybe for Phil and who knows who else? And certainly for her own family and the stronger person she was becoming for them.

Thanks, Lord, for pushing me through that filthy metal door. If I hadn't gone through it, I'd never have found out what you had here for all of us.

---

1. Think of everything you have read about Katherine Fraley's story. What good results have come because

Katherine trusted the Lord and relied on his grace?

---

2. What good results have come because you have trusted the Lord in difficult situations?

 GOD'S WORD FOR US
Read Esther 7:1 — 8:2.
Background: In a wonderfully-told story in 5:9 — 6:14, Haman plans to get rid of Mordecai even before the appointed time. In fact he plans to have Mordecai executed the next day. Instead he winds up having to publicly honor Mordecai! Meanwhile the king's order and Esther's second invitation are still pending.

---

3. During the second banquet, Esther judged that it was time to make her appeal. The moment the king signed the edict (3:8), he thought it was to his advantage to annihilate the Jews. How did Esther build her case, step by step, that it was not to the king's advantage (7:3-4)?

---

4. What would have shocked the king about Esther's words, "grant me my life" and "spare my people" (7:3)?

5. What would have happened to Esther and Mordecai if the king had still sided with Haman?

6. When have you been glad that you identified yourself with God's people?

7. Haman had thought he was on top of the world—except for the bothersome detail of Mordecai, and the king's order would soon take care of that. Now everything was changed. Haman must have known his number was up when the king left in a rage. What did Haman do as a last resort, and with what results (7:7-10)?

8. What rewards came to Esther and Mordecai (8:1-2)?

Summary of the rest of the book of Esther: Xerxes granted Esther's request. Since a Persian king's edict could not be altered, the only way for the king to stop the slaughter of the Jews was with a counteracting edict. Xerxes issued another order giving the Jews "in every city the right to assemble and protect themselves" (8:11). The Jews received the order with joy, and because of the Jews' new status in Persia, people of other nationalities even converted to Judaism (8:16-17). The Jews got the upper hand over their enemies. Their victory is celebrated in the feast of Purim (9:26) from the word *pur*, or "lot," because Haman cast the lot to determine the day they should be destroyed.

---

9. In what situation(s) are you especially eager to see God's faithfulness?

---

10. Where might you be overlooking signs of God's faithfulness?

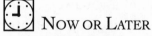 NOW OR LATER

☐ Faced with the need to state her case, Esther bided her time; but she didn't wait forever. In what ways is the Lord asking you to state your case, which is actually his case?

☐ Prayerfully consider your strategy for saying the right words in the right place at the right time. It's not unspiritual to have a game plan; Esther certainly had one when she went to the king and then put him off through two banquets. Like Esther, we cannot predict how our hearers will receive our words. Our job is to restrain ourselves when the time is not yet, then speak and act at the right time, trusting God. As you consider your options, write the specifics as a prayer here:

"Lord, I have to appeal to _____ for _____ or on behalf of _____.

I'm afraid that_____. Please help me know_____, and give me the right words to _____.

Thank you for standing with me in this."

☐ In your own way, whether verbally, in symbols, out loud, silently, alone or with others, offer your praise and thanks to the Lord for his faithfulness. Let the evidence of his faithfulness which you have seen lead you to trust him for the evidence you have not yet seen.

☐ For further study of a wise appeal, read Philemon. In his brief letter to a master on behalf of a runaway slave, Paul showed himself a master at making a diplomatic appeal.

☐ For further study of seeing God's faithfulness, read Acts 16. When Paul and his companions were frustrated in their attempts to enter certain areas, the Holy Spirit moved them to go to Philippi, where a strong church was started—the church to whom Paul later wrote Philippians.

Guidelines for Leaders

My grace is sufficient for you. (2 Corinthians 12:9)

If leading a Bible study is something new for you, don't worry. These studies are designed to be led easily. As a matter of fact, the flow of questions through the passage from observation to interpretation to application is so natural that you may feel that the studies lead themselves.

You don't need to be an expert on the Bible or a trained teacher to lead a Bible discussion. The idea behind these inductive studies is that the leader guides group members to discover for themselves what the Bible has to say. This method of learning will allow group members to remember much more of what is said than a lecture would.

This study guide is flexible. You can use it with a variety of groups—student, professional, neighborhood or church groups. Each study takes about forty-five minutes in a group setting with the possibility of extending the time to sixty minutes or more by adding questions from "Now or Later."

There are some important facts to know about group dynamics and encouraging discussion. The suggestions listed below should enable you to effectively and enjoyably fulfill your role as leader.

Preparing for the Study

1. Ask God to help you understand and apply the passage in your own life. Unless this happens, you will not be prepared to lead others. Pray too for the various members of the group. Ask God to open your hearts to the message of his Word and motivate you to action.

2. Read the introduction to the entire guide to get an overview of the subject at hand and the issues which will be explored. Also read through the introductions to each study to get the flow of the continuing story that runs through the guide and to get familiar with the characters. Be ready to refer the group to the list of characters on the back of the contents page if they have questions about the story.

3. As you begin each study, read and reread the assigned Bible passage to familiarize yourself with it.

4. This study guide is based on the New International Version of the Bible. It will help you and the group if you use this translation as the basis for your study and discussion.

5. Carefully work through each question in the study. Spend time in meditation and reflection as you consider how to respond.

6. Write your thoughts and responses in the space provided in the study guide. This will help you to express your understanding of the passage clearly.

7. It might help you to have a Bible dictionary handy. Use it to look up any unfamiliar words, names or places. (For additional help on how to study a passage, see chapter five of *Leading Bible Discussions*, InterVarsity Press.)

8. Take the "Now or Later" portion of each study seriously. Consider how you need to apply the Scripture to your life. Remember that the group will follow your lead in responding to the studies. They will not go any deeper than you do.

Leading the Study

1. Begin the study on time. Open with prayer, asking God to help the group to understand and apply the passage.

2. Be sure that everyone in your group has a study guide. Encourage the group to prepare beforehand for each discussion by reading the introduction to the guide and by working through the questions in the study.

3. At the beginning of your first time together, explain that these studies are meant to be discussions, not lectures. Encourage the members of the group to participate. However, do not put pressure on those who may be hesitant to speak during the first few sessions.

4. Have a group member read the story in "Setting the Stage" at the beginning of the discussion or allow group members some time to read this silently. These stories are designed to draw the readers into the topic of the study and show how the topic is related to our daily lives. It is merely a starting point so don't allow the group members to get bogged down with details of the story or with trying to make a literal connection to the passage to be studied. Just enjoy them.

5. Every study begins with one or more "approach" questions, which are meant to be asked before the passage is read. These questions are designed to connect the opening story with the theme of the study and to encourage group members to begin to open up. Encourage as many members as possible to participate and be ready to get the discussion going with your own response.

Approach questions can reveal where our thoughts or feelings need to be transformed by Scripture. That is why it is especially important not to read the passage before the approach question is asked. The passage will tend to color the honest reactions people would otherwise give because they are, of course, supposed to think the way the Bible does.

6. Have a group member read aloud the passage to be studied.

7. As you ask the questions under "God's Word for Us," keep in mind that they are designed to be used just as they are written. You may simply read them aloud. Or you may prefer to express them in your own words.

There may be times when it is appropriate to deviate from the study guide. For example, a question may have already been answered. If so, move on to the next question. Or someone may raise an important question not covered in the guide. Take time to discuss it, but try to keep the group from going off on tangents.

8. Avoid answering your own questions. If necessary, repeat or rephrase them until they are clearly understood. An eager group quickly becomes passive and silent if they think the leader will do most of the talking.

9. Don't be afraid of silence. People may need time to think about the question before formulating their answers.

10. Don't be content with just one answer. Ask, "What do the rest of you think?" or "anything else?" until several people have given answers to the question.

11. Acknowledge all contributions. Try to be affirming whenever possible. Never reject an answer. If it is clearly off-base, ask, "Which verse led you to that conclusion?" or again, "What do the rest of you think?"

12. Don't expect every answer to be addressed to you,

even though this will probably happen at first. As group members become more at ease, they will begin to truly interact with each other. This is one sign of healthy discussion.

13. Don't be afraid of controversy. It can be very stimulating. If you don't resolve an issue completely, don't be frustrated. Move on and keep it in mind for later. A subsequent study may solve the problem.

14. Periodically summarize what the group has said about the passage. This helps to draw together the various ideas mentioned and gives continuity to the study. But don't preach.

15. "Now or Later" can be used in a variety of ways depending on the time available to you and the interests of your group members. You may want to discuss an application question or idea and make some commitments. Or you may want to allow five minutes or so of quiet reflection within the group time so that people can journal their responses. Then, ask simply, "What did you experience (and/or learn) as you journaled?"

You will want to use at least one of these ideas to wrap up the group time, but you may want to encourage group members to continue working through other ideas throughout the week. You can continue discussing what has been learned at your next meeting.

16. Conclude your time together with conversational prayer. Ask for God in following through on the commitments you've made.

17. End on time.

Many more suggestions and helps are found in *Small Group Leaders' Handbook* and *The Big Book on Small Groups* (both from InterVarsity Press). Reading through one of these books would be worth your time.

Study Notes

Study 1. The Grace of Inner Beauty. Esther 2:1-14.
Purpose: To focus on our inner relationship with God in contrast to the world's focus on externals.

Question 3. "This decree demonstrated the prevailing attitudes toward women in ancient Persia. By abducting young virgins from all over the empire, Xerxes issued a painful reminder to all his subjects about the 'proper' behavior of women — and the supremacy of his own will" (*The Quest Study Bible* [Grand Rapids, Mich.: Zondervan, 1994], p. 667).

Question 4. When the Babylonian king Nebuchadnezzar conquered Jerusalem in 587 B.C., he exiled thousands of Jews east to the vicinity of Babylon in what is now Iraq. A hundred years later, after Babylon had fallen to the Persians, it was the home of Esther. Since the death of her parents she had been raised by her cousin Mordecai. Though she had never seen her Palestinian homeland, Esther knew and kept her identity as a Jew and one of God's people.

Question 6. Though you may not have faced the same literal situations, look for similarities in feelings and obstacles. For example, have you felt emotionally "orphaned" because significant people who should have cared for you were not there when you needed them? Have parts of your life been dominated by other people whom you didn't choose? Have you been thrust into alien surroundings where no one shared your morals and you became an object of ridicule for your beliefs?

Question 7. God gave Esther special favor in the eyes of Hegai, the man (probably a eunuch) who was in charge of the harem. Not only did he provide her with the best possible physical situation, we detect that he respected her as well. God also enabled Mordecai to have access to the area and learn in judicious ways how Esther was doing.

Question 8. Focusing on the internals might be easy for a day or two, but this was a full year of lavish beauty treatments with a dramatic year-end goal always in mind—meeting and pleasing the king. That prospect must have been alternately terrifying and exciting. At times a woman might retreat to her inner self as a welcome escape from the superficiality; at other times she might give in to the flattery and glamour of it all.

In some ways Esther's problem is not far from our problem. We are immersed in a culture which prizes, even worships, externals. The cover of every slick women's magazine, no matter what serious articles it has inside, is dominated by the image of a glamorous young woman. External female beauty sells practically every product on the market. Developing our inner beauty can feel like a second-rate effort, a sort of poor consolation for not having enough outer beauty.

Question 9. Esther had little help from outside to keep herself focused on eternal realities. Concentrating on her inner self and her relationship with God would take continuous conscious effort. Faithful prayer would have comforted her and given her strength. (Her prayers were no doubt silent because she had still not risked revealing that she was Jewish.) Though she possessed no written Scriptures, she must have known the stories of how God delivered his people from their enemies time and again. She also knew God's laws, which told her how to relate to the people around her in ways that reflected God's character. Above all, she had the presence of God himself. He stayed faithful to her in his concern for her inner holiness—just as he stays faithful to us.

Study 2. The Grace of Consistency. Esther 2:15-23.

Purpose: To consider the value of consistent Christian character and the risks it may require.

Question 3. "The biblical account of Xerxes (Ahasuerus) has been corroborated by historians. The picture given in the book of Esther of a king who was a despot and thoroughly sensuous in character corresponds with the account given by the Greek historian Herodotus. He greatly enlarged his harem at Persepolis, as excavation shows, and became involved in a shameful affair with his brother's wife and later with the daughter as well. The description of the ornate palace with its bright curtains is quite in the manner of the gaudy palaces of the Persians. Excavations at Susa . . . have yielded abundant evidence of the rich ornamentation of the walls of the palace and of the richly colored glazed bricks used there" (J. A. Thompson, *The Bible and Archaeology,* 3rd ed. [Grand Rapids, Mich.: Eerdmans, 1982], p. 220).

Question 4. Over the preceding year Esther had obviously established a trusting relationship with Hegai, who was in charge of the harem (v. 8), because she took with her only what he suggested when she was finally taken to the king. We are not told whether she initially trusted the king, who saw her at first as only a prize possession, but she apparently had enough respect for him to save his life. She put full trust in her adoptive father Mordecai; he obviously trusted her also when he told her about the conspiracy. She did not trust anyone with the fact that she was Jewish (v. 20).

Question 6. Xerxes realized that Esther was loyal to him and valued his life—she could have let him be assassinated but chose to save him. He also saw that she did not seize the credit for herself but unselfishly gave credit to Mordecai.

Question 7. No matter what Esther and Mordecai thought of Xerxes personally, they showed compassion on him by saving him from being murdered over a spiteful grievance. They also had considerable stake in the stability of Xerxes' position. Esther's fate (at least humanly speaking) was in Xerxes' hands, her situation was still very new, and the king was volatile (recall how speedily he deposed Vashti). Mordecai had some position of leadership or honor "at the king's gate" (v. 21), either from previous service or because of his connection with the new queen. Both Esther's and Mordecai's lives were bound up with the fate of Xerxes.

Question 8. When we are having difficulty relating to someone, the Lord often gives us an opportunity to choose to show compassion for that person. Our sinful tendency is to turn away from the opportunity or neglect to even see it. Instead we should make use of it, because through it the Lord can begin to change our attitudes and build a new bridge of communication with that difficult person. Our actions also give that difficult person a chance to see us differently.

Study 3. The Grace to Stand for God. Esther 3:1-11.

Purpose: To determine to trust God and remain faithful to him in the face of opposition.

Question 3. Esther was made queen in the seventh year of Xerxes' reign (2:16). It is now his twelfth year as king (3:7). The book of Esther does not tell all that happened during the intervening years, but obviously Mordecai was now in a place of influence at the king's gate, where judgment was given. Mordecai was different in both behavior and nationality, and Haman clearly understood that the two distinctives were inseparably connected.

Question 4. Some commentators say that Mordecai's refusal to bow to Haman stemmed from the traditional hostility between the Jews and the Agagites, going back to 1 Samuel 15, when against God's orders King Saul spared Agag the king of the Amalekites. It is also possible that Mordecai refused to kneel because for him that sort of reverence was reserved for God. He may also have been making a statement about Haman's character, since he knew that Haman did not deserve to be honored, no matter what the king thought.

Question 5. "In his unreasoning fury Haman plans the destruction of an entire race. Superstition insists he must choose a 'lucky day.' And fortunately for the Jews it was eleven months off" ("Esther," in *Eerdmans' Handbook to the Bible*, ed. David Alexander and Pat Alexander [Grand Rapids, Mich.: Eerdmans, 1973], p. 314).

Question 7. Consider the reactions you get when you tell people you are a Christian. If they have bad impressions of Christians, whether from personal experience or stories they have heard, they tend to lump you in with all "those" people (narrow-minded, judgmental, hypocritical, anti-intellectual or whatever stereotype they have). In such situations we can only pray that the Lord gives us a chance to counteract those impressions and prove ourselves over time. We should also be very careful not to do anything to confirm our new friends' bad impressions.

Question 8. When we hear Christians criticized, we should always give the criticism a fair hearing. Maybe some of it is legitimate! God can use the blunt evaluations of non-Christian critics to show us where we need to change.

Study 4. The Grace to Take Risks. Esther 4:1-14.

Purpose: To develop courage to obey the Lord when he puts us in a particular situation and singles us out for a difficult job.

Question 3. In Jewish custom, tearing one's clothes was (and still is) a sign of grief. David tore his clothes when he learned Saul was dead (2 Samuel 1:11). Tamar tore her robe and put ashes on her head after she was raped by her half-brother (2 Samuel 13:19). The high priest Caiaphas tore his clothes when he heard what he considered blasphemy from Jesus (Matthew 26:65). Wearing sackcloth and ashes signified mourning and repentance.

Question 4. Distressed by Mordecai's behavior, Esther wanted to ease his pain, but she didn't yet know what was wrong. Knowing he had enemies in the palace, she may have wanted to keep him from calling unnecessary attention to himself.

Question 5. There is an urgency and insistence in each of Mordecai's actions. He told the servant Hathach every detail of Haman's plan, gave him a copy of the order to give to Esther, and told Hathach to urge Esther to go to the king. Already Mordecai had decided Esther was the one to intervene to save the Jews, and he was not reticent about telling her so.

Question 7. It has often been pointed out that the book of Esther does not include the name of God. But God's purposes and care run throughout the book, and Mordecai's words in verse 14 are one of the strongest instances, when he tells Esther, "who knows but that you have come to royal position for such a time as this?" Mordecai did not flatter Esther about her persuasive powers or speaking ability. He simply told her she was the chosen one and did not speculate on why. Mordecai was absolutely convinced of the purposes of God in Esther's being in that place at that time.

Question 8. Some other possibilities: I feel flattered. I wonder why the other person thinks I'm the one. I feel proud. I hope somebody else will do it.

Question 10. It is not egotistical to recognize what God has done through us, things which would not have happened in just that way if we had not been in that place at that time. Those events should lead us to celebrate what God has accomplished and resolve to continue being where he wants us to be.

Study 5. The Grace to Have Courage. Esther 4:15—5:8.

Purpose: To determine to go ahead and act as God leads us in spite of our fear.

Question 3. Though prayer is not mentioned, we can assume that Esther's fast included intense prayer to the Lord. "Spontaneous fasts on occasions of distress or mourning . . . could be means of earnest supplication proclaimed by a leader in the community. . . . and undoubtedly continued also to be a means by which the community besought the divine compassion at times of calamity" (H. H. Guthrie Jr., "Fast," in *The Interpreter's Dictionary of the Bible*, Vol. 2 [Nashville, Tenn.: Abingdon, 1962], p. 243).

Question 4. Although Esther accepted the fact that she was the chosen one, she did not go into the task as a loner. She asked for and counted on help from the entire Jewish community in the city of Susa. Her request for help tells us something about the humility of godly leadership.

Questions 5-6. There is an abandonment about Esther's statement, but not the abandonment of resignation or despair. She placed in God's hands not only her appeal to the king, but her own physical life. While Esther did not wish for her own death, she valued obedience to God more highly than preserving her life. She would go to the king and try to save her people, and she would leave to God what happened to her personally. Her faith was in God rather than in the king or in her ability to persuade him.

Question 7. Other possible responses: I am usually quite decisive. I wish I were more decisive. I tend to exaggerate too many things into crises. I should deal with situations earlier before they become crises.

Question 8. The king held out his gold scepter as a sign that Esther was accepted and could enter the court. If he had withheld that sign, Esther would have died for entering his presence unsummoned (4:11). The gold scepter was the undisputed sign of the king's authority.

Two main types of scepter are pictured in ancient art: a long, slender staff with an ornamented head; and a

short-handled battle mace, with a pear-shaped stone
head three or four inches long. The first is seen in a
relief of the Persian king Darius [father of Xerxes],
grasped in the right hand a little below the tip and with
the butt resting on the floor between the king's feet. (L.
E. Toombs, "Scepter," in *Interpreter's Dictionary*, Vol. 4,
p. 235.)

Study 6. The Grace to See God's Faithfulness. Esther 7:1—8:2.

Purpose: To look for evidence of God's faithfulness in all
the events of our lives.

Question 2. Of course you can't know all the good results
that have come about. Some results you may see later,
some you may never know about. Consider the ones that
God has allowed you to see and enjoy.

Question 3. Esther reminded the king that she had found
favor with him (as evidenced in his extending the scepter
to her, repeatedly promising to grant her whatever she
asked, and coming to her banquets). Still she politely used
the conditional word "if" (v. 3), allowing the king an out.
First she asked for her own life. She knew that the king
would be shocked to learn that his queen's life was in
danger, and he would be ready to do anything to defend
her. Then she asked for the lives of her people, identifying
herself with the Jews who were marked for slaughter.
Aware that the Jews, a conquered and captive people,
were held in low esteem by the Persians, she made it clear
that she was asking for no special treatment, only for her
people's lives.

Question 4. Up till now the king had no idea that Esther
was Jewish. While male Jews had the sign of circumci-
sion, there was no physical evidence to indicate that a

woman was a Jew.

Question 5. As Jews they would have been included in the genocide. Mordecai had already sensed that the king would not make an exception just for his queen (4:13-14).

Question 7. "The king's response has been variously characterized by scholars—excessive, drunken, a cruel jest, unreasonable, and so on; but one must remember that in antiquity very strong feelings and strict regulations centered on the harem. . . . Had Haman knelt so much as a foot away from the queen's couch, the king's reaction could still have been justified" (Carey A. Moore, "Esther," *The Anchor Bible*, Vol. 7B [Garden City, N.Y.: Doubleday, 1971], p. 72).

InterVarsity Press Bible Studies by Sandy Larsen

Women of Character Bible Studies
A Woman of Creativity
A Woman of Grace

LifeGuide® Bible Studies
(with Dale Larsen)
Faith
Hosea

Teamwork Discipleship Guides (with Dale Larsen)
Starting with Christ
Maturing in Christ